Grubs
and Other Garden Pests

TEXT BY ELAINE PASCOE

PHOTOGRAPHS BY DWIGHT KUHN

BLACKBIRCH PRESS

An imprint of Thomson Gale, a part of The Thomson Corporation

Detroit • New York • San Francisco • San Diego • New Haven, Conn. • Waterville, Maine • London • Munich

LIBRARY OF CONGRESS CATALOGING-IN-PUBLICATION DATA

Pascoe, Elaine.
 Grubs and other garden pests / by Elaine Pascoe; photographs by Dwight Kuhn.
    p. cm. — (Nature close-up)
 Includes bibliographical references and index.
 ISBN 1-4103-0536-8 (hardcover : alk. paper)
 1. Garden pests—Juvenile literature. 2. Insects—Experiments—Juvenile literature. I.
Title II. Series: Pascoe, Elaine. Nature close-up.

 SB603.5.P37 2005
 635.9'27—dc22   2005002206

Printed in the United States of America
10 9 8 7 6 5 4 3 2 1

Contents

Pests!

Every spring gardeners plant flowers and vegetables. And every year insects and other hungry critters move in to feed on the plants. The battle between people and plant pests has been going on as long as people have been growing crops.

The insects and other animals that people call pests aren't out to do harm, however. They're just going about their business, trying to survive. By planting groups of the plants pests eat, gardeners set up perfect conditions for garden pests. You can't blame them for taking advantage of the garden "cafeteria."

A huge variety of animals can be pests in gardens, from tiny **mites** to **mammals** such as rabbits, raccoons, and even deer. In this book you'll read mostly about insect pests. Insects attack every part of garden plants, from roots to shoots, flowers, and fruits.

Root Eaters

When green lawn grass turns brown in patches and the grass can be pulled up easily, chances are that white grubs have been at work. If you peel back a section of sod, you may see them. They look like fat white worms, curled into a C shape. But they're not worms. They're grubs.

Grubs are wormlike insect **larvae**, or undeveloped young. The white grubs that infest lawns are the larvae of scarab beetles. Scarab beetles include Japanese beetles, June beetles, and other types.

A June beetle grub makes a meal of grass roots.

5

SNAILS AND SLUGS: SLIMY PESTS

Silvery trails of slime—and holes in leaves—are signs that land snails or slugs have been in the garden. These animals love the tender leaves, shoots, berries, and vegetables that they find in gardens. But you may not see them unless you look for them. They are mostly active at night. During the day they hide in damp, shady places.

Snails and slugs belong to a group of animals called mollusks. They have soft bodies, with no bony skeleton. A snail is protected by its hard shell, made of calcium and minerals that the animal secretes. A slug has no shell. Both animals secrete lots of slimy mucus. The mucus keeps them from drying out. It also smoothes their way as they slowly creep along, looking for food.

A land snail or slug has two pairs of feelers on its head. The animal's eyes are set at the tips of the longer pair. The shorter pair is located near the mouth, which is on the animal's

A land snail lays its eggs in a garden.

underside. The mouth has a rasplike organ called a radula, which is used to file off fine particles of food.

Because the chemicals that kill snails also kill other animals, gardeners usually find other ways to control them. They pick them off plants by hand or catch them in baited traps. Sometimes they keep these pests off plants with copper barriers, which react with snail slime. Getting rid of debris where snails and slugs can hide during the day helps, too. Snakes, birds, and frogs are among the predators that eat slugs and snails.

Land snails and slugs reproduce in an unusual way. They are hermaphrodites. This means that they have both male and female characteristics. When two snails mate, they exchange sperm. Each snail then lays a cluster of eggs. When the young snails hatch, they look like miniature adults.

Slugs love strawberries and other fruits.

The grubs hatch in summer from eggs that female beetles lay in soil. At first they are small and feed on grass roots close to the soil surface. But they soon begin to grow. Like all insects, a grub has a tough outer skin, or **exoskeleton**, instead of an inner skeleton like yours. This skin doesn't grow. So, as the grub grows, it must **molt**. It sheds its old skin and steps out in a new, bigger one.

A close-up of a grub's head shows its chewing mouthparts.

An adult June beetle looks nothing like the grub.

The grub molts several times, growing larger and eating more roots. When the weather turns cool, the grub moves deeper in the soil. It spends the winter there. In spring it crawls back toward the surface. After feeding on roots for a short time, it begins the next stage of its life. It sheds its skin once more and becomes a **pupa**. As a pupa, the insect is **dormant**. It does not eat or move. But its body changes. When the change is complete, the pupa casing splits open and an adult beetle crawls out of the soil. It looks nothing like the larva.

An adult Japanese beetle is oval, with a hard, coppery green shell. Like all insects, it has six legs and three body parts—the head, **thorax**, and abdomen. It also has two pairs of wings. Only the hind pair is for flying. The front wings form a protective covering for the hind wings. They flip out of the way when the beetle takes off. The adult also has **compound eyes**, with many lenses, and strong mouthparts for chewing food. Antennae located on the head help it taste and touch its world.

An adult Japanese beetle chews a leaf of a garden plant.

Root maggots feed on roots in garden soil.

Adult Japanese beetles feed on roses and other garden plants. But most other scarab beetles are not pests as adults. They do damage only as larvae. The larvae of many other insects attack plant roots, too.

Root maggots are the larvae of certain flies. They attack specific crops, such as sugar beets and canola. The adults look a lot like common houseflies. The larvae are small, white, and legless. They hatch in summer from eggs laid in the soil. After feeding on roots, they spend the winter in the soil. In spring, they pupate and crawl out of the soil as adult flies.

When grubs and maggots feed on plant roots, they cut the plant's supply of water and nutrients. This weakens the plant and makes it easy for plant diseases to take hold. If there are lots of grubs, they may eat enough roots to kill plants outright. But because the grubs stay in the soil, you may know they're there only when you see the damage they've done.

Weevils and More

The beetles are a big insect group, and they include a lot of plant pests. Many of these pests eat leaves and other plant parts instead of—or in addition to—roots. Adults as well as grubs do the damage.

Weevils belong to a group of beetles called snout beetles. As adults, they have teardrop-shaped bodies and long snouts, with mouthparts at the tip. Many are quite small, just $1/4$ inch (6mm) or so in length. But they can do a lot of damage to plants. Like most garden pests, weevils usually specialize in certain plants. For example, strawberry root weevils mostly feed on berry plants. The grubs eat plant roots, and the adults feed on leaves and fruits.

This beetle's long snout marks it as a weevil.

America's most famous weevil is the cotton boll weevil. Adult cotton boll weevils feed on the buds and blossoms of cotton bolls, or seed pods. They lay their eggs in the plant's bolls, where cotton fibers develop. When the larvae hatch, they eat the cotton. In the early part of the 20th century, cotton boll weevils destroyed cotton crops throughout the South and forced many farmers into bankruptcy.

The Colorado potato beetle is a specialist, too. As you'd guess from its name, this insect feeds on potato leaves. But it will also go for tomato, eggplant, and pepper plants. Adult females lay their eggs on the undersides of leaves. Each female can lay 500 or more eggs in a month! The eggs hatch in four to nine days, and the grubs begin to eat as soon as they hatch. They are full-grown grubs in just two to three weeks. Then they climb down to the ground to pupate and come out five to ten days later as adult beetles.

A potato beetle has laid her eggs (left) on the leaves of a potato plant.

13

A striped cucumber beetle eats the petals of a cucumber flower.

Because they grow so quickly, there can be several generations in a single growing season. Adults spend the winter dormant in the soil and come out to feed again in the spring.

The Mexican bean beetle is another common pest. Adults and grubs eat the leaves and sometimes the pods and stems of bean plants. Melons, squash, and cucumbers attract different beetle pests: striped and spotted cucumber beetles. Adult cucumber beetles feed on the leaves and stems of those plants. As they feed, they help spread several plant diseases. The grubs injure plants by feeding on the roots and tunneling through stems. Tiny flea beetles look (and jump) like fleas, but they are not related to those insects. These beetles feed on a variety of vegetables and berries. Adults eat leaves, and grubs eat both roots and leaves.

An adult bean beetle crawls through the petals of a string-bean flower.

15

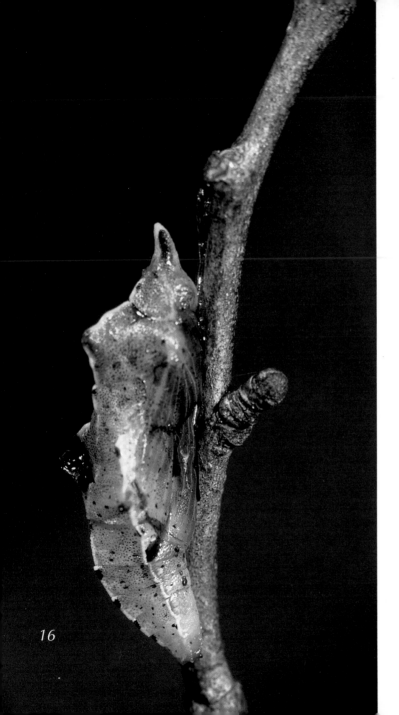

Leaf Chewers

Butterflies and moths feed mostly on flower nectar and don't harm plants. But their larvae, or caterpillars, are not so welcome in the garden.

The cabbage white butterfly was imported from Europe to eastern Canada in the mid-1800s. Since then it has spread throughout North America. Its caterpillar, called the cabbage worm, is a serious pest of cole crops—cabbage, cauliflower, broccoli, kale, collards, and related plants.

The caterpillars are velvety green with faint yellow stripes. They hatch from eggs that female butterflies lay on the leaves of host plants. The caterpillars munch away at the soft plant tissue between the large veins and ribs of the leaves, leaving the leaves riddled with little holes. They slowly work their way into the center of the plant. Like other insect larvae, they molt as they grow. In about two weeks they are full grown, about an inch (2.5cm) long. They are then ready for their next life stage.

A cabbage worm changes into chrysalis (left) on its way to becoming an adult butterfly.

Adult cabbage white butterflies feed on flower nectar.

The cabbage worm attaches itself to a stem or some other handy object with a little blob of silk that its body produces. It molts again and emerges as a pupa, or **chrysalis**, with a hard outer shell. Inside the shell, it changes into an adult butterfly. The change takes just a week or two in warm weather. But in the fall, when the weather turns cold, the insects stay in the pupa stage. Adults appear in the spring, ready to mate and lay eggs.

Caterpillars of other butterflies and moths feed on different plants. Some are famous for their big appetites. One gypsy moth caterpillar can eat up to a square foot (929 sq. cm) of leaves a day! These caterpillars mainly eat tree leaves. In large numbers, they can strip sections of forest bare.

Hungry Hoppers

The champion leaf eaters are grasshoppers. These insects live mostly in grassy fields, but swarms of hungry grasshoppers can make short work of farm fields and gardens. They have even been known to chew up laundry hung outside to dry!

There are two big groups of grasshoppers: short-horned and long-horned. Short-horned grasshoppers have antennae shorter than their bodies. Their ears are located on the abdomen, just behind their long hind legs. Long-horned hoppers have slender antennae as long as or longer than their bodies. Their ears are on their front legs. Both kinds have powerful hind legs for

Gypsy moth caterpillars are nonstop eaters.

Swarms of short-horned grasshoppers, like this one, can do serious damage to crops.

leaping into the air and two pairs of wings for flying. They have strong, chewing mouthparts and five eyes—two large compound ones and three tiny simple eyes, including one in the middle of the forehead.

Grasshoppers hatch from eggs as **nymphs**. They look like tiny adults, but they have no wings. A grasshopper nymph can eat up to twice its body weight each day, and it grows fast. It molts as often as once a week. After four to six molts, it is a winged adult.

The most serious pests, including locusts, are in the short-horned group. When conditions are right, some of these grasshoppers can multiply into enormous swarms. The swarms migrate over wide areas—nymphs hopping, adults flying—devouring crops and pastures. Pioneers in the American West described swarms that darkened the skies and stretched for miles. Grasshoppers are still a problem for farmers today.

Most long-horned grasshoppers don't cause so much trouble. They include katydids, which you may hear "singing" on summer evenings. Long-horned grasshoppers "sing" by rubbing their front wings together. Most short-horned kinds rub their hind legs against the front wings. Usually only male grasshoppers make sounds.

Sap Suckers

Many garden pests feed by sucking juices from plants. These insects pierce the outer wall of a stem or leaf with a short, sharp beak, called a **proboscis**. Then they suck up the juices inside. By stealing water and nutrients, they cause the plant to wilt. They often also spread diseases as they move from plant to plant.

Aphids are tiny insects, most no bigger than the head of a pin. There are many different kinds, and they feed on many kinds of plants. You'll often find them clustered on stems and under leaves. Aphids suck in more plant juices than they can use. After filtering out the nutrients they need, they excrete the rest as a sugary substance called honeydew.

A grasshopper nymph looks like a small wingless adult.
Inset: Pinhead-sized aphids suck sap from plant stems.

Above: An aphid gives birth to live young.
Below: Scale insects have a protective waxy coating.

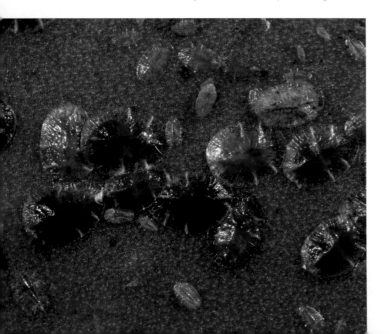

These insects have complicated life cycles. Wingless aphids hatch from eggs in the spring. They are all females, but they can reproduce asexually—without mating. They produce a generation of wingless daughters, which are born live. These daughters in turn give birth to daughters of their own. Finally, as cold weather nears, winged males as well as females are produced. They mate, and the females lay eggs that hatch the following spring.

Aphids belong to a big group of sap-sucking insects. Other plant pests in this group include leafhoppers, whiteflies, mealybugs, and scale insects. Scale insects are covered with a protective armor of waxy material. Females have no wings, and many even lose their legs and antennae when they become adults. These small insects spend their lives in one place on a host plant, drinking sap.

Squash bugs are also sap suckers. They feed on squash, pumpkin, and other vine plants. They suck sap from the leaves and stems, causing the vines to wilt and wither. Female squash bugs lay their eggs on the undersides of the leaves of host plants. The insects hatch as nymphs and go through several molts before they are adults.

Adults can live through cold winters by hibernating under plant debris and in other sheltered places.

Thrips are tiny sucking insects, less than $\frac{1}{8}$ inch (3mm) long. They may be yellow, brown, or black. Different types feed on leaves, buds, flowers, and small fruits. It's easy to see the damage they do—dried, wilted leaves, buds that fail to open, deformed flowers. It's harder to see the tiny thrips. You can shake them off the plant onto a sheet of white paper and use a magnifying glass to identify them.

Thrips, shown much enlarged, feast among flower petals.

Fighting Garden Pests

Grubs in the lawn, caterpillars in the cabbage, bugs on the squash, aphids on the roses—what's a gardener to do? Often the answer is, "Nothing." If there are only a few of the insects, healthy plants probably won't be harmed. One of the best defenses against insect pests is to buy sturdy plants and keep them healthy, by giving them good soil and the right amount of water.

When pests begin to multiply, however, they may damage plants. Farmers and gardeners often use chemical **pesticides** to control insects. These chemicals must be used very carefully. Some can harm other animals, and many kill all insects that come in contact with them.

You might think that getting rid of all the insects in a garden would be a good thing. But you'd be wrong. Insects do more good than harm in the garden. In fact, many flowering plants could not survive without them. Insects such as bees and butterflies come to flowers to feed on nectar, a sweet substance deep in the heart of the flower. As insects or other pollinators push into the flower to get the nectar, they pick up grains of **pollen**, which contains the plant's male sex cells. When they move on to the next flower, they carry the pollen along. Grains of pollen brush off on the **pistil** of the new flower. This begins the process of seed formation.

Other insects are **predators** that help control plant pests. Lacewings, ladybugs, damsel bugs, mantids, flower flies, and assassin bugs catch and eat aphids and other pests. Tiny parasitic wasps attack some insect pests, too. These wasps lay their eggs in a host insect. When the eggs hatch, the wasp larvae feed on the host insect and kill it.

These **beneficial** insects often find their way to gardens. So do spiders, birds, toads, and other animals that eat insects. People can also buy predator wasps, ladybugs, lacewings, and mantids (or their eggs) and turn them loose in the garden. They can also apply sprays containing bacteria, fungi, or microscopic worms called nematodes that infect specific pest insects.

There are other ways to discourage garden pests. One is to clean up dead plants and debris in the fall. This takes away sites where pests can shelter through the winter. By using these natural methods of pest control, people can limit the use of chemicals that harm the environment.

A bumblebee flies to a tomato flower. If the bee pollinates the flower, a tomato will develop.

2

Collecting and Caring for Cabbage Worms

In any garden, you are sure to find some pests. In spring and summer, check plants for insects and look for damage that pests have done to leaves, fruits, and flowers. You can learn a lot about these animals just by watching them as they feed and go about their business. A field guide will help you identify the different insects you find, and a magnifying glass will help you study them close-up.

The cabbage white caterpillar, or cabbage worm, is a good subject for closer study. You can catch these caterpillars and keep them for a while, so you can watch them over time.

This chapter will tell you how to collect and care for them. You'll also find out how to raise the caterpillars from eggs that you can buy through the mail.

Collecting Cabbage Worms

Look for cabbage worms in spring and summer on crops such as broccoli, brussels sprouts, cabbage, cauliflower, collards, and kale. Take along a jar or similar container for collecting any that you find. The jar should have a lid in which holes have been punched to let air in. Ask an adult to help with this. Or you can cover the jar with mesh, held on with a rubber band.

When you find a cabbage worm, break off the part of the plant with the caterpillar on it. Put the plant part, caterpillar and all, into your jar, and cover it. When you bring the caterpillars home, set up a container for them.

Cabbage worm larva.

What to Do:

1. Push toothpicks through the side of the container at several spots.

2. Wash the brussels sprouts and peel off the outer leaves, to be sure there are no traces of pesticide on them. Ask an adult to help cut the sprouts in half. Then stick halved brussels sprouts on the ends of the toothpicks in your container.

3. Put a piece of paper towel on the bottom of the container.

4. Carefully move the cabbage worms from your collection jar to their new home. Put them right on the brussels sprouts.

Cabbage worm larvae on halved brussels sprouts.

5. Cover the container with mesh, held on by a rubber band.

6. Every day, change the paper towel to get rid of caterpillar droppings. Put in fresh halved brussels sprouts; the old ones will begin to dry out and spoil after a day or so.

29

Cabbage Worms from Eggs

You can buy cabbage white butterfly eggs from some biological supply companies (see page 46). If you give them the right conditions, they will hatch into cabbage worms.

The newly hatched grubs feed on tender seedlings, so you will need to grow some plants for them. Use fast-growing plants such as radishes and turnips. Plant the seeds at least five days before you expect the eggs to arrive, so the grubs will have food when they hatch.

Cabbage worm eggs.

What to Do:

1. Place a layer of sand or pebbles in the bottom of the container. Cover with soil mixture.

2. Mix the radish and turnip seeds, and plant them in the soil. Dampen the soil with water.

3. Place the container under bright light to allow the plants to grow. Make sure the soil stays evenly moist, but not soggy. A good way to do this is to mist the soil with a spray bottle as soon as it starts to dry out.

4. When the eggs arrive, they will be on a strip of waxed paper in a small plastic vial. Use tweezers to carefully lift out the waxed strip and place it egg-side down on the plant seedlings. Do not touch the eggs!

5. Keep the container and eggs in a warm, draft free place. As the caterpillars get bigger, you can feed them brussels sprouts as described under "Collecting."

Above: Radish and turnip sprouts. Below: Cabbage worm eggs on plastic tape, placed on seedlings.

From Caterpillar to Butterfly

In two weeks or more, the cabbage worms will be full grown. Then they will move to the side or top of their container. There each worm will form a chrysalis. You can continue to watch the insect develop, but you will need to move the chrysalis to a screen cage or some other sort of butterfly home.

You can make a screen cage with wire screening from the hardware store. Roll the screen into a tube, and fasten it with staples at the top and bottom. Use cake tins to make the top and bottom of the cage.

You can use a large cardboard carton, too. Ask an adult to help you cut out a big window on all four sides of the carton. Cover the openings with screening or netting, taping or stapling it in place. The top can be taped shut after the insects are inside.

Now you are ready to move the chrysalis to the butterfly home.

Cabbage worm chrysalises on the edge of a larva container.

32

What to Do:

1. Carefully remove the chrysalis from the cabbage worm container.
2. Put a small piece of double-sided tape on the base of the chrysalis.
3. Gently attach the tape to the twig. Be sure the chrysalis faces upward—the wide end is the top, and the thinnest part is the tail, which should point down.
4. Prop the twig in your butterfly home.

Adult butterflies usually appear after a week or two. They feed on flower nectar. Put a bouquet of fresh flowers, in a container of water, in their home. Add fresh flowers whenever the old ones begin to wilt. Since cabbage white butterflies are pests, it's best not to release them.

A screen home for adult butterflies.

3

Investigating Garden Pests

Although gardeners don't like to see pests on their plants, many of these animals are fascinating to watch. On the following pages, you'll find activities that will help you learn more about some of them, including grubs, caterpillars, and slugs. Try to disturb the animals as little as possible as you do these activities. You'll learn the most about them if you let them behave naturally.

Are Garden Pests Picky Eaters?

You can find pests of many kinds in a garden, on plants of many kinds. Do pests prefer specific plants, or will they go for whatever plant is nearby? Decide what you think, and then do this experiment to find out.

What You Need:
- Potato beetle grub, cabbage worm, or similar pest
- Leaves from garden plants
- Jar or other container to hold leaves

What to Do:

1. Find a potato beetle grub, a cabbage worm, or any other leaf-eating crawler in the garden. Collect it as described in chapter 2.

2. Take some leaves from the plant on which you find the pest. Take leaves from several other garden plants, too. Note which leaves come from which plants.

3. Put the leaves together in a container of water, and put the insect on the leaves. The leaves should be touching each other, so the insect can crawl from one to the next.

Results: Which plants does your pest prefer? Try this experiment again, using different leaves or a different pest. Do you get the same results?

Conclusion: What do your results tell you about what your insects need to survive?

What Plant Parts Do Cabbage Worms Like to Eat?

Cabbage worms like broccoli and similar plants. What parts of the plant are they most likely to eat—stems, leaves, or buds? Make your best guess, based on what you have read about these insects. Then do this experiment to find out.

What to Do:

1. You can use broccoli from the market for this activity. Make sure the piece you use has some side shoots with leaves. Wash the broccoli first.

2. Put the broccoli in a small container and add the cabbage worms. Use a spoon to move the worms into the container.

3. Cover the container with mesh and a rubber band. Check frequently to see where the cabbage worms go.

Results: What parts of the plant do most of the cabbage worms prefer?

Conclusion: What do your results tell you about the type of damage that cabbage worms do in a garden?

Will Sunlight Affect the Hatching of Cabbage White Butterfly Eggs?

Female cabbage white butterflies lay 50 or more eggs that hatch in two to ten days. Will sunlight speed up the hatching? Decide what you think, and then do this experiment to see if you are right.

38

What to Do:

1. Follow the instructions in chapter 2 to set up your container and grow food plants before adding cabbage white butterfly eggs.

2. You can buy the eggs from a biological supply company. They will come attached to a piece of paper. Cut the paper in half, so you have two pieces with eggs on each.

3. Put the eggs on the plants in your container, as described in chapter 2. Place one paper on a leaf exposed to the sun. Put the other on a leaf that is shaded, so the sunlight isn't directly on the eggs.

4. Check often, using a magnifying glass to see if the eggs have hatched. The eggs on each leaf will all hatch at about the same time.

Results: Note if the two groups of eggs hatch together, or if one group hatches first.

Conclusion: What do your results tell you about the conditions that are best for egg hatching in the wild? Can you think of other factors that could affect egg hatching? How would you design an experiment to test those factors?

What You Need:

- Slugs or snails
- Radish or bean seeds
- Small aquarium or similar container
- Soil
- Sand
- Mesh and a rubber band, to cover the container

Will Sand Keep Slugs at Bay?

Some gardeners believe that a barrier of sand will help keep slugs away from plants. Because sand is dry and rough, they think, slugs won't want to cross it. Does it work? Make your best guess, and then do this activity to find out.

1. Put a layer of soil in your container, and plant some radish or bean seeds. Put the container in bright light, and keep the soil evenly moist.

2. After the seeds sprout, thin the seedlings. You want two groups of plants, spaced so that they do not touch each other or the sides of the container.

3. Put sand around the base of one plant. Leave soil around the base of the other.

4. Add some slugs (or snails) from the garden. Cover the container with mesh and a rubber band.

Results: Watch to see where the slugs go.

Conclusion: Based on your results, is sand a good slug barrier? Try the experiment again, using different materials as a barrier. You can use ashes or diatomaceous earth, which is sold in garden stores.

More Activities with Garden Pests

1. Take an insect safari in your garden or a nearby park. See how many kinds of insects you can find. Your library or school may have field guides that will help you identify the insects. Are these insects pests, or do they help the garden?

2. Get close to a grub. Use a magnifying glass for a close-up look at a grub or caterpillar. How does it move? How does it eat? Does it have eyes or antennae? How many legs? Make a sketch of your insect, and write down your observations.

3. Find a plant infested with insect pests, such as cucumber beetles or potato beetles. Pick off all the pests. (You can kill them by dropping them into a cup of soapy water.) See if new pests come to the plant and, if so, how long it takes.

4. Put predators to work in your garden. In early spring order mantid (praying mantis) egg cases from a biological supply company, such as those listed on page 46. Place the egg cases in your garden. After warm weather comes, check them each day in late morning or around noon to see if the young mantids have hatched. Ladybugs and lacewings are other insect predators that you can buy and set loose in your garden.

Results and Conclusions

Here are some possible results and conclusions for the activities on pages 35 to 41. Many factors may affect the results of these activities. If your results differ, try to think of reasons why. Repeat the activity with different conditions, and see if your results change.

Colorado potato beetles: larva (left) and adult with eggs.

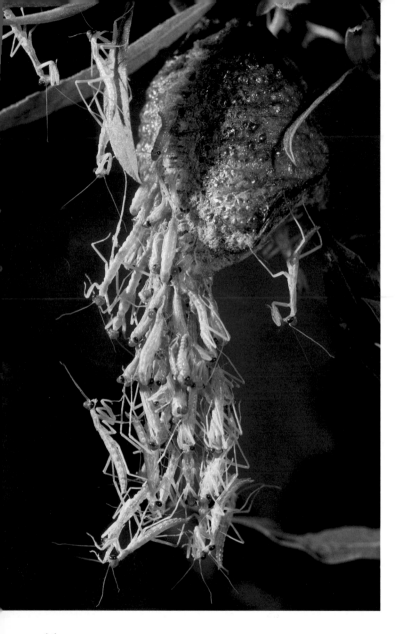

Are garden pests picky eaters?

Many garden pests will eat only certain plants. Our potato beetle grubs preferred potato and tomato leaves. These insects are normally found on potato plants. But they also eat the leaves of related plants, including tomato and pepper plants.

What plant parts do cabbage worms like to eat?

Our cabbage worms preferred the buds and leaves to the stems. These insects usually eat softer plant tissues. When feeding on cabbage, broccoli, or cauliflower, they often crawl toward the center of the head, which is tender.

Will sunlight affect the hatching of cabbage white butterfly eggs?

Your results may vary. Often the extra warmth of sunlight helps the eggs hatch faster. But in strong sunlight, eggs may dry out and fail to hatch at all.

Will sand keep slugs at bay?

We found that slugs went across the sand without any problem.

Mantids hatch from their egg case.

Some Words About Garden Pests

beneficial Helpful.

chrysalis A butterfly pupa.

compound eyes Eyes that have many lenses, or facets.

dormant Inactive.

exoskeleton The hard outer skin of an insect. It takes the place of an internal skeleton.

larvae The immature forms of some insects. Larvae generally do not look like the adult forms.

mammals Warm-blooded animals that feed their young milk produced by the mother.

mites Tiny relatives of spiders.

molt To shed the skin.

nymphs Immature forms of certain insects. Nymphs often look like adults without wings.

pesticides Chemicals used to kill insect pests.

pistil The female part of a flower.

pollen A fine powder that contains a plant's male sex cells (sperm).

predators Animals that kill and eat other animals.

proboscis A sharp beak that certain insects use to pierce and suck.

pupa The stage during which an insect changes from a larva to an adult.

thorax The center section of an insect's body. Usually the legs and wings are attached here.

Japanese beetle adults.

Sources for Grubs and Other Garden Pests

This source has cabbage white butterfly (Pieris rapae) eggs and mantid egg cases:

Carolina Biological Supply Company
2700 York Road
Burlington, NC 27215
(800) 334-5551
www.carolina.com

This source has mantid egg cases:

Science Kit and Boreal Laboratories
777 E. Park Drive
PO Box 5003
Tonawanda, NY 14150
(800) 828-7777
www.sciencekit.com

Earworm on corn.

For More Information

Books

Mel Boring, *Caterpillars, Bugs and Butterflies*. Chanhassen, MN: North Word Press, 1999.

Jinny Johnson and Jimmy Johnson, *Simon & Schuster Children's Guide to Insects and Spiders*. New York: Simon & Schuster, 1997.

Sally Kneidel, *Pet Bugs: A Kid's Guide to Catching and Keeping Touchable Insects*. Hoboken, NJ: John Wiley & Sons, 1994.

Robin Kittrell Laughlin and Sue Hubbel, *Backyard Bugs*. San Francisco: Chronicle Books, 1996.

Melissa Stewart, *Maggots, Grubs, and More: The Secret Lives of Young Insects*. Brookfield, CT: Millbrook Press, 2003.

Christina Wilsdon, *Insects* (National Audubon Society First Field Guides). New York: Scholastic, 1998.

Web Sites

Get This Bug Off of Me! (www.uky.edu/Agriculture/Entomology/ythfacts/stories/hurtrnot. htm). Tips for identifying common harmful and harmless insects.

Insectclopedia (www.insectclopedia.com). Learn about insects, including common pests in lawns and gardens.

Kid's Valley Garden (www.raw-connections.com/garden). Kid-friendly tips for planting and maintaining a garden, including controlling slugs and insects.

Index